# PEGGY POND CHURCH
# NEW & SELECTED POEMS

## Ahsahta Press

Boise State University
Boise, Idaho

Versions of some of these poems were first published in *Foretaste, Familiar Journey, Ultimatum For Man, The Ripened Fields* and in *Survey Graphic Magazine* and *Southwestern Review.*

For permission to reprint poems previously published by Sunstone Press, grateful acknowledgement is made.

ISBN 0-916272-02-8

Library of Congress Catalog Card Number:
75-29917

# Contents

Preface

## I.   from **Foretaste** (1933):

## II.   from **Familiar Journey** (1936):

## III.   from **Ultimatum for Man** (1946):

# IV.　New Poems:

# V.　from **The Ripened Fields:**

# Preface

A reader can trace the influence of landscape upon a poet whether the background of the poetry consists of lakes and mountains, or city towers and slums. Poetry must have a setting, and the excellent poet is one who relates the scenes for poetic dramas to action and to characters, not for color and decoration. Poems are always dramatic, since a poet must concentrate upon himself and others, or upon himself with others.

Peggy Pond Church has written many of her poems in the settings of mesas and mountains as they mark the scenery of northern New Mexico where she was born on December 1, 1903, and where, except for her school years, she has spent the greater part of her life. In **Foretaste** (1933) she writes: "I have been part of earth's beauty in moments beyond the edge of living." Such lines as "the black rain on silver days," sheep described as moving up a slope "like a grey cloud" and "yellow fruit spread to the sun" make this book refreshing to both mind and eye.

Of **Familiar Journey** (1936) the poet Haniel Long remarked in a personal letter to the author, "It is a fuller picture of a Being, a Life, than any I know in contemporary letters. The three aspects of our sentience—environment, personality, racial memory—are in a really wonderful balance. The triple harmony you have woven here makes a music as sane and sound as it is lyric." The subject of the book is love, considered not as something that belongs to any one of us, but a road we travel, a ritual journey, an ancient pilgrimage.

**Ultimatum For Man** (1946) is a right-angle turn for Mrs. Church, a turn not away from the landscape line, but an adjustment to a new point of view in which the poet sees individuals as units in a social group. In 1943 the Los Alamos Ranch School, a preparatory school for boys where her husband taught for more than twenty years, was taken over by the United States government for the nuclear physics laboratory which was to design the atomic bomb. Mrs. Church refers to the scientists as men who worked against great odds, secretly and often at night, to construct a weapon which moved "in terrible, malevolent beauty" both to save and to destroy. William Rose Benét, reviewing the book for the **Saturday Review of Literature** in 1946, remarked, "Mrs. Church's poetry is distinctly of this time, the work of a fine human being, concerned with the terror of the hour."

A group of fifteen sonnets entitled "The Ripened Fields" was reprinted as a pamphlet in the fall of 1954 after they had been published in a Quaker Quarterly called **Inward Light.** The sonnets detail the contests between minds and hearts sealed by the contract of marriage. The series begins in defiance which is sustained by reflection, but ends in the discovery that love may set a single course however far the paths may wander back and forth. Only the introductory poem is here reprinted.

A poet's career is a journey made in despite of himself. His experience as a writer is a journey in directions he cannot predetermine. The reader of Peggy Pond Church's poetry will join her in a search for beauty and understanding of both nature and humanity.

T. M. Pearce
University of New Mexico
September 17, 1975

# I.   from **Foretaste** (1933)

# Sheep Country

In spring the sheep are driven over the mountain
While there is still snow knee-deep in every shadow
And the wind's edge is sharp in the Valle country.
The sheep come up from the canyons
Like a grey cloud.  They move slowly.  They leave unnibbled
Not a low-growing leaf, not a sliver of grass,
Not a flower.

In Capulin canyon the river crossings are muddied
Before the wild choke cherries are in flower;
There are a hundred twisted trails on Rabbit mountain
Made by the sheep that come up from Peña Blanca,
From Cienega and Cochiti, from Santo Domingo,
From the dirty corrals, from the flat, dusty mesas
Where they have fed all winter.

I have seen them going up Santa Clara canyon in April
When Tsacoma mountain is still a white cloud of brightness
Lifted against the sky; when the wind is bitter
And there is only a haze of green around the aspens
You can see by looking slantwise, never directly,
Never in a second glance, never by coming closer.

I have seen the sheep move up Santa Clara canyon
And over the ridge
And down the Rito de los Indios and onward into
The long, curved Valle San Antonio.

And I have seen the names of the sheepherders written
On the aspen trees halfway up Tsacoma
And on Redondo mountain where the aspens fight for their rootholds
In the black rocks, in the frozen lava.
Casimiro Chaves, I have seen written; Juan Pino; Reyes Contreras;
From Chamita and Abiquiu and Española,
Nambé and Pojuaque.

These are the names of boys, carved here and written,
Whose wits, they say, aren't fit for any other work,
Or men whose minds are still the minds of children;
Who do not desire anything more of living
Than to lie in the glittering shadow of an aspen
On the rim of the Valles where the sheep feed
And move downward slowly.

There are men who desire much more and find much less.
Must we all be madmen, I wonder, or innocents,
To follow the sheep along the ridge of the Valles,
Looking down, west, to the sea of grasses,
    The far-off, tangled, grass-hidden threads of water,
And the nets of rain through which the farther mountains
Shine like a shadow?

# Open Winter

Spring will come
After a while to these tired, these snow-starved hills;
These hills that have known no rest the whole long winter;
These hills that have lain
Under the pale, under the comfortless sky
Like a sleeper whom sleep has cheated.
Spring will come
Like a too early, a too persistent daylight
After the long, unrestful night and sleepless.
The trees will wearily once more put on their leaves,
The grass lift slightly.
The tired flowers will blossom one by one.
But the whole summer will be only a heavy-lidded
Waiting for autumn,
For a second winter,
Not like this one, never again like this one;
A winter of deep snow, of snow-heaped branches,
Of snow so deep along the ground not the earliest violet
But will sleep dreamlessly nor wake till April.

# Alien

I can never be one of them.
The forest will be friendly for a day;
The trees for a little while will be familiar
Suffering me to walk among them,
And I can lean on a rock and watch the water
Eating a way through harsh earth to its ocean.

But the trail bends.
The leaves turn dark in a shadow
And I remember that earth here once in anger
Spewed burning rock out of that close-glimpsed mountain
And that there is no one here who speaks my language,
Not tree, nor stone, nor time-oblivious river.

# Winter Sketch

Today there is snow all over the valley,
And we ride in a little world hidden from
    the mountains.
The hills behind Pojuaque that are usually
    painted on the sky
The color of fire against the color of mountains,
Tonight are hyacinth pink on a grey cloud curtain,
Fading to violet, fading to no color at all.
And there is a house with a blue door and a
    blue-framed window
Like a reminder of the sky, and a lamp lit in it;
And three pigs; and a cow chewing her cud
    in a dooryard.
Finally only the noiseless, invisible snow pricking
    down out of darkness.

# Peach Trees

Do not hurry past this orchard too quickly
Saying:   Yes, surely, that is a beautiful thing.
As though the moment of flaming were the
        purpose of this orchard
Accomplished now that your all-claiming eyes
        have seen it.
Remember that before these trees were ever planted,
A thin, small, unprotesting beast of burden
Dragged a curved plough through the reluctant earth,
With a man stooping behind in the hot sun to
        guide it.
Remember a wide ditch had to be dug here
        to coax the river
Up the dry, stubborn flanks of these hills, a
        long time barren,
And that a woman, ageless as the brown
        hills are ageless,
Hoed the difficult earth about the young roots planted,
And dreamed, before ever the slender branches
        had budded,
Of yellow fruit spread to the sun in her dooryard
        in autumn.

# Abiquiu—Thursday In Holy Week

Is there any way I can be sure to remember
Abiquiu?
How the sun went down suddenly
Behind the hills, and the river darkened.  Everything
Became sound only laid upon silence
    where had been lately
Bright houses and people moving past them,
    and dogs and children.

The moon was a long time coming up.
It came up slowly.
The hills grew tall and terrible before it.  The long mesa
Behind Abiquiu was a huge blackness, growing blacker
On the slow silver sky.
The fields had been ploughed a little and we stumbled
    through them
Guiding our steps by grasping the budding willows
Beside the acequia.  We didn't belong here.
This wasn't our world.  We should never have come
    here at all.
We shivered and laid our lengths along the border
Of the field, a wall of low stone.  The trail from
    the morada
Went past that wall.  We heard something wailing
High in the hills.  We waited.

A little beyond midnight they came out of the morada
And went past the wall, three of them, one singing;
One with the pito, the Penitente flute that is
    more sorrowful
Than any sorrowful sound that was ever uttered
In music.  The third man marched
With body bent a little forward.  At the end
    of each line of singing
He brought the woven whip across his shoulders
With a lashing sound, rhythmical, like an accent;

A sound that was dull and harsh, as though already
Blood softened the lean back.   A lantern flickered
In the hand of the singer.   Its swinging shadow
Was swallowed soon in darkness.

I, under the cold stars, there in the cold night, watching
This greatest of remembered tragedies enacted
By men who as soon as Easter was over
Would go back to their ordinary way of living—
To the fields they must finish plowing and sowing;
To the sheep that would be lambing soon in the canyons;
To the ditches that must be cleared to flood
        the orchards,
Each man when his turn came, from the mother
        acequia—
Men whose brown, wind-lined faces I had often
        seen passing
In wagons loaded with wood brought down
        from the mesas

Behind Abiquiu, or driving burros
Slowly, as if in some other country, along the highway.
I, crouched there against the cold stone, prone
        on the cold earth, listening;
Thought:   There is something they know, these men,
        that we have forgotten;
They remember, here in these mountains, here
        at Abiquiu on this spring night,
On this unforgettable Thursday before Easter,
That to imitate simply, unaware even of any
        special meaning
A great and tragic action, is to be lifted by it
For a moment out of commonplace living
        toward greatness.

# After Looking Into A Genealogy

Time is not, when I remember you, my grandmothers.
Your bones, your flesh have gone into the dust;
From granite stones the wind has wiped your names.
The years have trod your graves flat with the earth,
You who were beautiful, you who died still young
In childbirth, you who saw
Ninety and more full years before you passed,
Whose husbands died at sea, whose husbands died
In the stern winters of a wilderness.

Time is not, when I remember you, my grandmothers.
Mercy and Lydia and Abigail,
Ruth and Mehitable; sea-captains' wives,
Daughters of soldiers, mothers of men of God;
Statira, Betsey, Patience, Margery,
Remember, whose other name the gravestones have
        forgotten.

Out of old books these names, from moldering stones,
All that is left of you, my grandmothers!
        All but the blood
That makes me one with you.  The blood that cried
Like a wanderer returned when I first saw—
I, the desert-born, this offspring
        of New England growing
Among New Mexico mountains—when I first saw
The dogwood blossoming in Connecticut woods,
The meadows sprinkled with a rain of daisies,
The apple-orchard set in low, green hills.

I know now why in my dreams I had seen those hills
        and had remembered
The covered bridges over Vermont rivers,
And why, whenever I came upon a clearing
        in mountain country
I thought:  One could build a house here.
That slope would make a pasture.  An orchard
        would be fruitful
In a few years, and the apples fragrant.
The butter I'd churn would be cool and sweetened
In a stone house over this mountain-spewed
        thread of water.

When I was a little girl
My mother kept the milk in a house
    built half underground
With shelves around the walls.   There the warm milk
    yellowed
With heavy cream in rows of shallow pans.   Something
    familiar,
Something not remembered first stirred in me
When I crept down to watch her.

But most of all, my grandmothers, your blood leaps
    in me
(Obliterating time, making of me one person with my
    forebears,
One person who has lived since life crawled up
    from the waters
And became man, who will not die
Till the last woman of this race is barren)
Most of all, my blood stirs with your voices
When the winds of winter thunder like ocean water
And the white snow whirls down in utter darkness.

Then I remember, or it seems as if I remembered,
The earliest winter, and the fierce grey water
Heaped between us and England (the grey water
Cradling more than one of my grandfathers)
The desperate stand we made against that winter,
The bitter battle.

We were sturdy-limbed, the daughters of that winter.
We had inherited strength that must be tried.
    We could not
Live and grow old, unrestless, in security,
And so we went off, shoulder to shoulder with our men,
    and singing,
Into the farther wilderness.

In these days, my grandmothers, the weak live easily.
The weak crowd out the strong like weeds
    in an untilled garden.
Where can we go, we in whom your blood sings?—
The eager blood of our forefathers, of our foremothers,
    who marched chin forward
And always toward the horizon?

# I Have Looked At The Earth

And you said: I am afraid to have you fly.
Had you forgotten that afternoon on Point Lobos
When, because the tide of centuries that had swept over
    those rocks somehow washed over us with the sound
    of unceasing water, and because there was so much
    life there in the color of tree-shadowed sky and voices
    invisible and not human,
We said that the more we could be aware of the world,
    of the color and sound of it, of its taste in our mouths
    and the feel of it under our fingers,
The more we could perhaps remember and recognize and
    regain of its beauty
After death had stripped us of our familiar tools for seeing
    and listening and touching?
We thought, for the space of an afternoon, with the
    thought of rocks.  The deep heart of the earth,
    muffled and unhurried, sounded through us.  We
    almost took root there, forgetting we were human and
    mortal, becoming earth there at the sea's edge.

When we are dead we know this one thing will become
    of us:
We will go into the ground; our bodies will surely
    crumble and feed tree-roots, or blow as dust on the
    wind or be rain-washed at last into ocean.
Is it this you fear for me, bidding me not fly, bidding
    me go carefully and save this body?

If there were any more danger in flying than always in
    living, when death hangs ever invisible above our
    heads, and we never know at what instant the
    thread will be cut that holds it,
Would it be so dreadful to drop, in an interval of ecstasy,
    in a fear-escaping second, out of this human existence,
    to go back to earth and be one in the constellations,
    to give birth to mountains, to be intimate
    with the tide and the rain and the seasons?

I have known these moments of unlimited happiness:
That afternoon on Point Lobos that was like going home
    out of an alien country;
A moment on Tsacoma Mountain where the tides of the
    air are shattered like waves and become clouds, and
    go down as rain on the sea-forgotten valley;
And that moment of flying over the Mojave.  The pain
    of death at that moment would not have been greater
    than my heart bore at beholding earth naked and
    virgin, with the shadow of twilight above her like
    a lover.
Each of these moments was like a sudden dying, a brief
    escape from the body, an instant of being the beauty
    which, living, we only taste a little.
Oh never fear death for me for I have looked at the
    earth and loved it.  I have been part of earth's beauty
    in moments beyond the edge of living.

# II. from **Familiar Journey** (1936)

# Carved In Ivory

Carve this in ivory,
delicate hand of a dead craftsman!
Rise from the grave.
Stand upright,
bone upon unaccustomed bone.
Take shape, oh dust!
Remember, oh atoms of dust, the shape of the body.
Become a hand to carve this moment in ivory
so that it shall last forever,
leaf-shape, tree-root,
poise of a finger,
miniature pattern of flowers upon the garment,
even the shape the wind takes in the branches,
and the shape of love transfixed on the face of
        the lover.

# Alchemy

Strange when the essence of flowers
is indistinguishable from music.
Strange when music
blossoms like a flower
that can be seen as the blind see, only with the fingers.
Strange when the body
turns into bread and wine.

This is an alchemy
of which no alchemist would ever dream.
To change flowers for music,
music for stars,
stars for fingers,
body to bread,
bread into wine,
wine into god,
everything at last into love.

# We Spoke Of Love

We spoke of love by every usual name.
We said it was a bird, a song, a light,
the bread and wine of life, a cloud, a flame,
the scent of flowers upon the air at night.
Music we said it was, heard in a dream
no mortal might remember or forget.
It was the moving air, the flowing stream.
It was a sun that never rose nor set.
With countless names we sought to bind love fast.
We saw it float from every subtle snare,
leaving but shadow in each shape at last,
each tangible shape we built for it to wear.
At last we ceased to speak.   Then love became
the silence in our hearts and bore no name.

# For Rain

Let there be now
this day and this night of healing,
for you, for me, for the earth, for all who need it;
the quietness of rain to rest in,
rain on the roof,
rain on the leaves of the orchards,
rain on the round surface of water in the garden,
rain that shuts each dwelling in a shell of quietness,
a little cocoon of silence.
And let there be peace for us both, for the earth,
for all who need it,
the peace that lovers have at last and sleeping
shoulder to shoulder, oblivious of passion.

# No Other

What has flesh and blood to do
with this white world shaped of unbreathing crystal,
these mountains like an ethereal cold breath
blown on the colder sky?
Yes, we saw the red sun go down
and the white, frost-like wafer of the moon come up,
but our hearts were still sheathed in ice like the buds of the roses,
and I knew of no way to invoke the miracle
that would make a rose blossom in winter
or warm the cold snow,
or hasten the season for lovers who share no other
home than the green earth.

# This Ocean

All day we watched the ocean
heaping its white, incredibly brief blossoms
over the agony-veined, dark granite:
all day the green sea-water
thrusting into the rock clefts.

Seals basked,
barking at tide's edge,
swam, elusive as thought,
under the fluid marble .
surface of deep water.

Cypress
more ancient than memory
absorbed us into shadow.

I saw dead girls
bruise their white breasts
on the indifferent rock,
sea-sharpened, crystal, harder than diamond:
their long hair
netted the pale tide.

Darkness came down:
the gaunt sea-vultures
roosted, red-beaked
in the bleak rock.

I dared not touch you
with word or weight of finger:
your own gods claimed you, the elemental granite
bare at your heart's core.

Now I must take this ocean
into my own heart or be taken by it,
going down into it, naked and voiceless and
torn by the rocks like the drowned girls.

# Enchanted Mesa

Hard to climb:
the slow talus
yielding under the bent step:
the cleft in the rock where
the wind leaps
upward like chill flame:
swallows screaming.

Earth's weight
drags at the belly.
The heart soars.
Torn between
earth and clean air
we hang
clenched in hard rock.

Hand over hand now:
the blood roars
in the reluctant throat veins.
Do not look downward
onto the warm plain,
the level, the acquiescent
safe earth.

These perpendicular
weather-fractured cliffs of
sandstone intercept the
sharp sky.
The complacent
mind drags at the
winged heel.

But the bright edge
finally triumphs.
We stand fast,
erect in wind's path.
The waves of
time beat on the
sheer rock.

Swallows
protest our coming,
go past us like
arrows from a tense bow,
curved flight,
cleaving wind with
their sharp cries.

An hour on this
mesa escapes time.
Humanity vanishes,
becomes an unheard procession
on remote roads.   Only the strong
skeletal firmness of earth holds
sky on its shoulders.

Holds us also
that which we strove against
in climbing.
The heart soars
lifted upon its own roots.
Enchanted Mesa—
a winged rock rooted in the
spent plain.

# Familiar Journey

Back and forth on the same road
and the same hills.
I and the seasons going back and forth
on the same road; the orchards blossoming,
ripening their fruit, and the harvest gathered.
A new house is built and an old one
crumbles.   In the late nights
one window is sometimes lighted.
Who watches in silence
while an old man dies or a child is being born?
I and the stars go past
again and again on the same road.

The dark nights and the bright ones,
the summer days
with the clouds blossoming above the mountains,
tremendous flowers, white, and sheathed in purple
like the flowers of yucca;
and the meadow larks
with a song as cool as the fields of green alfalfa;
the cottonwood tree
at the curve of the ditch near Pojuaque
where the old men sit all day
and the young girls at night with their lovers,
the old tree that remembers
more than the oldest man in that village remembers
and that dies slowly now, withdrawing its shadow
a little every year.

And the luminous valley
where nothing grows but color,
blues, lavenders, violets,
and all the shades of rose seen in a sunset;

the long bluff like a wave,
a wave the color of a cloud at sunset,
a wave that never breaks,
transfixed forever at the moment of its breaking,
and the sharp spires like the bending crest of the wave;
the hills that go naked always to the sun,
naked to starlight,
clothing themselves in no shadow,
the remnants of ancient valleys,
fragments of canyon walls the wind and weather
have not destroyed yet,
secret valleys
only the sun and the wind know.

I going back and forth on the same road
as if it were another body that contained me;
and the great storms, the afternoons of sunlight,
the dark nights,
the mountains that are a flame on one horizon,
and the mountains like a blue, an incandescent shadow
rimming the west;

Familiar journey,
and the years of a life,
the happenings of a life
along this road like remembered hills,
like the valleys.

III.  from **Ultimatum for Man** (1946)

# Ultimatum for Man

Now the frontiers are all closed.
There is no other country we can run away to.
There is no ocean we can cross over.
At last we must turn and live with one another.

We cannot escape any longer.
We cannot continue to choose between good and evil
(the good for ourselves, the evil for our neighbors);
We must all bear the equal burden.

At last we who have been running away must turn and face it.
There is no room for hate left in the world we must live in.
Now we must learn love.   We can no longer escape it.
We can no longer escape from one another.

Love is no longer a theme for eloquence, or a way of life for a
        few to choose whose hearts can decide it.
It is the sternest necessity; the unequivocal ultimatum.
There is no other way out; there is no country we can flee to.
There is no man on earth who must not face this task now.

# Comment on a Troubled Era

We who spoil the earth for our own greed—
our forebears were more generous who watered it with their
    spent blood,

and the ancient inhabitants thereof who
stamped their prayers with their naked feet on the hard earth.

We forget the seasons control us still;
the seasons have not changed,
nor the rhythm of rainfall.

The moon that powerfully governs oceans,
governs the tides of our own blood.

This is inescapable;
and we are subject to the gravitational pull between planets,
the oscillations of starlight,

systole and diastole of the heart,
the double breathing,
the measured climax of love,
death and begetting.

This, my brethren, is all the law and the prophets.
Be still and know, or let the proud mind,
in subtle opposition, rend and destroy you.

# Poem to Accompany the Gift of a Loaf of Bread

I give you the ploughed field,
the smell of the moist earth,
the first shine of rainfall,
the full seed burst open;
the fragily groping
pale-fingered blind roots;
the green spear of living
thrust splendidly upward.
I give you the sun for a
summer's full season,
the cold shine of moonlight;
the wind tossing green waves;
the stir of the little mice
under this canopy
under these grasses.

I give you all men who have
shaped the furrow:
the sower, the reaper;
the factory worker
who founded the metal,
who fashioned the stern plough;
he who guided the thrasher.
I give you their toil and their
sweat and their heartbreak,
their despair and their courage,
their strength and their tenderness.
I give you the mill and the
song of the millers,
older than Egypt,
as ancient as hunger.

I give you the harvest,
the hum of the reapers,
the noise of the thrashers;
the warm grain poured out in a
great golden river;
give you the fine flour
moistened and sweetened;
salted and leavened;
stirred with humility,
kneaded with reverence;
give you the risen dough
warm to the shaping touch,
live as a beating heart
under these urgent and
listening fingers.

I give you the bread at last
fragrant as springtime;
fashioned of earth and sun;
sweet as a summer field,
good as the gentle rain,
golden as harvest.
*Take and eat,* saith the Lord,
*This is the sacrifice.*
*This is my body both*
*broken and offered.*
*This is the mystery.*
*This is the living God.*
*Feed on him in thy heart*
*by faith with thanksgiving.*

# Omens

I have seen omens in the sky,
and in the entrails of wild beasts slaughtered;
have felt the ground pulse without footfall;
watched dead leaves driven by no wind.

I know too how blood runs from the slit vein,
the bitter taste of blood on the lips,
the slow cup filling,
the sacrificial gesture;

have seen the hero strip himself of his armor
and come before me in the dark tent;
Oh beautiful body, naked and vulnerable;
I have held him defenceless through the long night

and have not shuddered when I saw him carried
under the knees and arms between two soldiers,
his lips clenched upon death, his head hung backward,
both eyes awake and staring at the dead sky.

On a heap of broken walls I have found the point of an
    arrow,
cold stone, vindictive, all that was left of hatred,
and a pot broken, all that was left of hunger.

# Epitaph for Man

What we had built with pride and toil,
with sweat and tears,
in our own massive fury we destroyed.
The splendid years
were shaken on us by our own blind hand.
Oh, who are they that from some tranquil star
after long time shall win them to this land,
shall beach themselves upon our ruined sphere,
and in what pity gaze
upon the desperate havoc of these days,
the blackened girder, the distorted steel,
the wild vine twining in the rotted wheel?

They shall take home no tale of living kind.
Strange, they shall say,
the race that wrought such things should pass away,
and all that bounteous and verdant earth,
rich-bosomed, with tall grass, so made for mirth,
such ample fields where men might toil and sing
shoulder to shoulder at their harvesting,
untilled now lies
beneath those beautiful and brimming skies.
No life moves there
and yet, far underground
we sometimes heard a furtive, creeping sound,
and hairless things that gave strange human cries
stared out at us with blind, vestigial eyes.

# The Nuclear Physicists

These are the men who
working secretly at night and against great odds
and in what peril they knew not of their own souls
invoked for man's sake the most ancient archetype of evil
and bade this go forth and save us at Hiroshima
and again at Nagasaki.

We had thought the magicians were all dead, but this was the
blackest of magic.
There was even the accompaniment of fire and brimstone,
the shape of evil, towering leagues high into heaven
in terrible, malevolent beauty, and, beneath, the bare trees
made utterly leafless in one instant, and the streets where no
one
moved, and some walls still standing
eyeless, and as silent as before Time.

These are the men who
now with aching voices
and with eyes that have seen too far into the world's fate,
tell us what they have done and what we must do.
In words that conceal apocalypse they warn us
what compact with evil was signed in the name of all the
living,
and how, if we demand that Evil keep his bargain,
we must keep ours, and yield our living spirits
into the irrevocable service of destruction.

Now we, in our wilderness, must reject the last temptation:
the kingdoms of earth and all the power and the glory,
and bow before the Lord our God, and serve Him
whose still small voice, after the wind, the earthquake,
the vision of fire, still speaks to those who listen
and will the world's good.

# Prelude to Act IV

Now we must learn again what the Greeks knew
and what all poets know.   The tragedy
unfolds before our pity-stricken hearts.
Watching, we weep for what we know must be.
Cassandra's voice still cries, the prophet's voice
doomed to speak truth and yet be unbelieved
until the fatal end.   Both blessed and cursed
by whom we have called gods, our destiny
is that of heroes who must always die
by their own mortal flaw.   No enemy
can doom us but ourselves, no god can save
though all the prophets shout their warning words
down Time's huge corridors.   So we must live
who are but men, and fight against the gods,
and never, though we know where safety lies,
swerve, seeking it, nor let the warning voice
dissuade us from our end.   The hero dies
true to himself, and all men weep for him
that he was great, and yet was vulnerable.
We live as man must live, who is both wise
and blind, who warned, yet never hears
the voice of his own wisdom, nor her tears.

# For the Hippolytus of Euripides

Like a gaunt pillar wreathed in weeping flowers
so stands in memory the afternoon
I first saw played the Greek Hippolytus.
Euripides, your ageless spirit stood
motionless at my side, and through your eyes
I saw the dreadful beauty of that doom
rise like a wave from the unfathomed sea
in which all passion sleeps. I saw it move
with gathering weight of agony and tears
upon that king and on that ravaged queen,
and on that lovely and ill-cherished youth
flung harsh on death. I heard the dark wave moan
and saw the delicate maidens lean like flowers
against the cold, the imperturbable stone.
Euripides, you knew what we must know
and what we dare not know: that life is stern
beyond our power to make it what we will,
and that the gods use men for their own ends,
and that the other face of love is hate.
That we can do so is what makes us men
and more than innocent flowers or mindless birds
that bloom or fly and perish without heed.
This is man's greatness, to behold his fate
unswerving as a wave, strong as the sea,
nor yet to stand aside, nor shield his eyes
but with his whole heart and with all his mind
to praise this beauty even though he dies.

# Vital Statistics

In 1710 my ancestor, William Cole,
died and was gathered to his fathers,
died and bequeathed his body to the earth,
his share of breath to air.
Follows this record of his worldly goods:

> *Imprimis:* A farm lot, 3 acres with a house,
> 3 roods of land by Nathaniel Rudd, his land,
> 30 acres of land lying near Mogory swamp.
> 1 feather bed with old tow tick, 2 coverlets,
> 2 bed blankets, 1 cheap bed tow tick,
> 1 great coat, 2 yards of new fine lining cloth,
> 1 grey mare, 1 roan mare, 1 yearling colt,
> 1 cow, 5 swine.
>
> 1 great chest, 1 small chest, 1 little box,
> 1 gallon jug, 1 warming pan, 1 frying pan,
> 1 great iron pot, 1 small iron pot, 2 pair of pothooks,
> 2 tubs, 1 spinning wheel,
> 3 chairs, 1 table,
> 1 highboy stand, 1 lowboy stand, 1 pair tow curtains,
> 1 gun, 2 powder horns,
> 1 bullet pouch, 1 pound of bullets,
> 1 pair of wool cards, 3 old pitchers and 1 bridle.
>
> 2 narrow axes, 1 hatchet and 2 pails,
> 2 washtubs, 3 cider barrels, 5 old tubs,
> 1 kneading trough, 1 grindstone and 1 bag,
> 1 barrel cider,
> a cradle, 1 old Bible, other books,
> 1 pound of woolen yarn.

This was the total wealth of William Cole,
the farmer and my forebear.
This is the shadow that his living flung
awhile upon the earth.   This is the shell
that was the creature's home.   The man is gone
leaving this little trace.   What tears he wept,
if, unashamed of tears, he wept at night,
my heart must guess whose blood once flowed in his
and knows the tenderness of men who march
against the world by day, who turn at night
to the strange warmth of woman by their side.

These goods could but equip the smallest house,
one room, one fire on which the two pots hung,
one window curtained against all outdoors.
In that one room his children were conceived
and cried into the world upon that bed.
This cradle rocked them all.

This is the shape of William Cole, his life,
the footprint in the sand that marked his stride,
the land he husbanded, the tools he used,
the smell of wet leaves on the wooded hill
and the game stalked for food.
This is the bridle hanging on the wall.
The red mare nickers and the grey looks up.
The harvest has been gathered from the field.
The juice of summer has been half-consumed
and who shall taste the rest?
The Bible that companioned him is closed
whereby he lived and moved beyond his time
in the immortal thought of men long dead
and deathless while he read.

Shaped too beside him in the moving air
the mother of his sons, his bride, his wife.
Her presence fills the room.   The spinning wheel
slows and shall turn no more.   The risen bread
shall not be baked for him.   He shall not wear
the great coat warmed with new fine lining cloth.
She was the root that nourished the green tree
and now the tree is fallen.   All its leaves
drop slowly one by one.

# IV. New Poems

# Peñas Negras

**May 30, 1948**

We walked in the early morning to the graveyard,
setting out before the sun had risen,
the flowers heavy in our arms, and the green blanket woven
by your loving hands to cover the grave of your mother.
This day, Corina, I came to know tenderness
that had long been buried in the graveyard of my own heart.

This morning I put aside my proud thought and walked beside you
to Peñas Negras, the valley of the black rocks,
and walked beside you, like a child, with my arms full of iris.
The meadowlarks sang, and the dew lay like a mystery on the tall grass.
The mountains were jewels of light on the cold horizon.
You knelt and plucked the wild grass from the grave and spread over it
    the blanket you had woven.
You set flowers at the head and the feet;
roses of paper among the petals of roses
bloomed upon the fallen crosses in the graveyard.

Oh I might have smiled at you once for this unreasoning gesture
of love toward the unliving.   Yet a spirit was incarnate
in your face and your pose as you knelt there, a wisdom of woman
that had been born of loving.   I saw how the maternal
is more than the flesh and the bones of the mortal mother.
Through my sudden tears I saw how your mother had taught you
from her place in your heart all that your child's heart needed
to make it a woman's.   Then I too knelt
and placed my flowers beside yours, and received this blessing.

*1948*

# Master Race

The mountain, ancient and wise as myth,
created prophecies above our city
enormous and unheeded.   Daily we witnessed
heroic marriages of light and darkness,
the births of heroes, the revolt of angels,
deities crowned and murdered, holy incests.
We were too proud to read unwritten wisdom.
We forbade any but our own tongue to be spoken.
Our knowledge had pierced all shrines and left them broken.

The former inhabitants whom we had made our servants
worshipped these wonders.   They spoke with delicate gestures
of a god in the cloud, in the rainfall.
They honored the earth as woman;
in winter would not permit a wheel to turn upon her.
They prayed with eagle's feathers, with the hand shaking yellow pollen,
with the sound of the drum hid deep in the earth like a heartbeat.
There were times when this stirred in us something long forgotten,
or a thing not dreamed yet.

We knew what we knew:
that the earth was nothing sacred;
that the voice of our brother's blood would not cry against us;
that whatever we wanted from women could be taken.
There was nothing joined that we dared not put asunder.
We did not fall on our knees when we rent the atom.
We could look upon God and live.   There was no wonder
our wisdom could not pierce in earth or heaven,
and claim for our possession.

When did the mountain cease to be our landmark?
When did we notice that our sky was barren?
When did a wilderness replace our marked roads?
We walked and seemed to stumble among ruins.
Stones, fallen, cried out in unfamiliar patterns.
Seeking, we could not find, hearing, all song was broken.
Our eyes did not weep for terror or for kindness.
We did not know at last whose children lead us,
nor if for scorn or pity of our blindness.

*1948*

# Even the Mountains Are Ripe

"Even the Mountains are Ripe" the Navaho have named September.
Even the mountains are ripe and for whose harvest?
For whom did choke cherry ripen?   Who tasted the warm red berries—
raspberries, strawberries, thimbleberries, fruit of the wild rose?
The pale grass arches to the wind's touch, springs back softly
under each delicate footprint where the deer move
light-footed as leaf-fall.   Birds bend grass blades;
strip seeds gently, speaking soft sounds of thanksgiving.
Joy! Joy! Joy! in delighted ascending cadence.
And what ear listens?
Aspens have ripened yellow
facsimiles of sunlight as though the bright sun
were begotten a thousands times in his own image.
Who shall gather and garner this treasure?
Where shall our hearts store this beauty?
—that which our minds have not thought, which our hands have not
    created?
Even the mountains are ripe, and who shall reap them?

*1948*

# Elegy For Another Day

Walking at evening along the edge of the loma
at the hour of daylight ebbing, the lamps being lighted,
I came past corrals where the tame beasts had been bedded,
stirring like children not yet asleep, left lonely.

The domestic fires of day dreamed down into soft ash;
only earth's west rim still glowed like an ember.
The twilight arch curved upward on the eastern
sky like the shadow of receding daylight.

Humans, companioned with one another in warm houses,
like bees hived in winter, had left the earth to silence,
as though sleep should heal the memory of violence,
as though maternal night made all things brothers,

as though earth had not received the blood of Abel,
as though men shared the breast of their one mother,
nor dreamed one might be loved above another,
nor fallen to quarreling yet who should be greatest.

A woman was standing, quiet, by the gate of the sheep pen
blessing with a last look the creatures she had tended,
alone and with peace in her eyes, the long day ended,
untired and strong like an eternal being

who knows her children will come home at evening
weary of warfare, all their weapons broken,
to sleep, to dream the word that must be spoken,
and wake perhaps embraced as still in dreaming.

*1948*

# Blue Heron

At the place where the canyon is wide and the river is shallow
and the sandbars are thick with cottonwood and rosy willow
I, driving around a bend in the road, and the world still in shadow,
    with my own eyes suddenly saw the blue heron fishing.

I was going too fast then to stop.  The sun had not risen.
The river was quiet and without color as a crystal prism
that has not caught light yet, and the heron was half hidden
    in a background of bare branches, yet I saw him fishing

immobile as though he had been rooted there forever
among the willows, long legs stretched and limber,
the serpentine neck poised, sheathed in quiescent feather,
    the live eye aware of the sky, and the road and the fish in the river.

Not moving, nor pursuing, but waiting in that stillness,
in the calm of the morning before the voices of children
shattered the air like glass, and men were driven
    against time and none could remember the blue heron fishing.

*1950*

# Elegy In Three Movements
# For Alice and Haniel Long
# I.

As they grew older—
he already half blind, she indomitably more frail
as though for his sake she allowed time to gnaw her only in secret—
we, knowing how she had been the tree
on which the vine of his life twined,
yes, twined and flowered with all its weaving tendrils
reaching with sensitive tips toward sunlight and moonlight,
had dreaded the inevitable death that must come to one of them
first in the fading of the long day's journey.
The leaves of their lives were so inextricably mingled
it seemed as though their roots must have become one root.

This was more true than we dreamed.
When the surgeon's last skill failed him
it was she who died first, as though they'd a common heart.
Though he was far from home, mysteriously knowing
that all was not well, she hurried ahead of him,
with a last effort of her exhausted will
upsetting even death's protocol
to make, if she could, the last darkness seem familiar
like a mother who lights her child to bed with a steady candle.

It was as though she being gone,
he still unknowing yet, began to bleed
his own sap back into the deep mulched earth
in which their roots were hid.
How shall we say it was not a happy ending
for two whose lives were joined into one music?
The last chords sound; the musician's hands fall slowly,
and every discord now resolves in silence.

# II.
# The Unicorn

I think he kept a unicorn
in his garden, or even himself was
partly a unicorn and reverted to the form at certain
seasons, or under the influence of the moon or
the scent of unidentified herbs,
or the echo of hoofbeats among the constellations
inaudible to most ears.

It was a difficult affliction
to bear with, the unicorn being
something unclassifiable, mythological,
not zoological in an age when
almost no one believes in mythology.
If Leda were to confess the swan rape or
Danae blame her condition on a
god in a ray of gold, you know what they's be called now!
So he was always careful to
hide the flaw in his heredity from the literal minded
who were often a bit puzzled
by the sharp rim of a hoofprint among the roses in the garden
or a tree rubbed by an aching horn.

As it turned out
he was in his most serious danger from maidens
who fancied they saw in him a resemblance
to something they had once dreamed of.
Their eager looks often threatened
to give him away, for he could never entirely
escape the unicorn's need of cooling its chafed horn
between their indulgent breasts.
There were few of them who understood they were dealing
with a legendary creature
who in his human form was undoubtedly
the most faithful and uxorious of husbands.

Married to a fat and
placid wife entirely preoccupied
as far as anyone could see with her sewing and ironing,
with a baby voice and almost no charm of conversation,
nevertheless it was to her he returned unfailingly
like the unicorn in the legend to the lap of the virgin.
Was she the antithesis of everything wild, I wonder?
Was it really she who kept him human?
Some thought it a pity but
what if the unicorn strain had won out?
Together they tamed it to live quite peacefully in the garden
among the cabbages and the roses.
Sometimes at teatime
I've thought I saw it curled between them like a good dog
whose quicksilver eyes laughed at us a little from a far world.

# III.
# Love Was Their Genius

"My wife maintained an air of calm and love"
Haniel Long

Love was their genius,
love presiding among us at the tea hour,
kindled over and over on the warm hearth,
reflected from their faces in the firelight.

Love was the air she maintained,
her content with being woman
and with his being man, his helplessness,
his strength where she had none.

Love was the old-fashioned motto she embroidered
for him like a child in cross-stitch;
it was the valentine he gave her,
his beating heart pierced by the silver arrow.

Love was the deaths he died
to all that was not love, over and over
yielding his vulnerable
flesh and his blood to the burning and the terror,

and coming back to find her steady presence
like daybreak in a dark room.
Love was the mirror
she kept unclouded for him.

Love was the lesson that they learned together
from flowers and earth and sun;
it was the cryptogram whose secret meaning
they read lifelong between them.

Love was the token they gave us,
the leaf on the path, the sentence underlined,
the flower pressed and hidden between the pages,
the curved shell left on the shore

for our hands to hold after the green wave slowly
dies back into the sea.

*1956*

# Still Life

A round plate on the breakfast table
holds in its white circumference
four colored stones,
a handful of sanddollars,
a twisted root washed up by the formless ocean.

Each morning she plays with them a little
like a child throwing jacks:
the mineral colors of the stones,
the rough sea-creatures,
the blind root shaped like something not yet human.

She cannot let them lie.
She cannot see the stones as only stones.
She says, "If these were birds and they could fly!"
and suddenly the air is full of birds;
the colors move and sing.

Sanddollars are sea-urchins,
urchins, echinoderms, are spiny skins;
the words are horror's kin;
her hair stands up
prickled with ancient dread.

There is a creature struggling in the root
to free itself.
Its voiceless agony
draws all her muscles taut.
Morning upon new morning brings no change.
The birds fly back into their stones again.

*1958*

# December

On a smoothed off hilltop
among the granite outcrops
I am sitting this December morning
observing among the random
and wrinkled stones at the base of a
juniper a colony of mushrooms
with caps the color of warm toast.

No bigger in circumference
than a dime and most of them
smaller, they are
gathered in clusters like a game of jackstones,
or like stars on the sphere of a
child's eye.

The sky is pale blue, the wind
like an invisible herd with horns in velvet
goes butting among the rough trees.
My skin rejoices
in the bright prick of winter,
warmth and cold joined
like a pair of
lively dancers.

The white dog, Poli-kota,
runs on spiralling errands in her loose flesh;
she is a collector of footprints,
of urinal smells draped over
bushes and low tree branches.
Her curled tongue
delivers damp messages
to my cold cheek.

She is unmindful of mushrooms,
treads them down blindly
as a quadruple disaster.
My heart cries
to think what like death
may someday befall our planet;
not anyone's purpose,
no one will mean to do it,
something random to us
as Poli among mushrooms.

Still
on this hillside
where dying and coming to life
go hand in hand together
I cannot mind long.
Here is a bone I have found,
perhaps a steer's vertebra
once hidden in gliding flesh.
Now weathered and whitened
it rests in my hand
like a wordless metaphor
in the shape of a butterfly.

*1961*

# Alas

Alas, my love I grow older.
The nights seem colder.
Morning no longer
sings me awake as it used to
with birds
or the sound of fish leaping.
The nets that I cast for my dreams
are torn and too heavy
to lift out of the draining water.

Day breaks
and I lie in my bed
like a chick
feeling my warmth curved
close as a shell around me.
There is frost on the window.
Ice crystals live and
growing into forests.
The sun will rise soon and melt them.
The slow fires that burn in my blood
even while I sleep, and keep it moving,
do not warm me as well as they used to.
The stars seem colder.

I do not dream of love any more,
only sometimes of death in deep waters.
What will it seem like, I wonder, not to waken?
The world will go on, I know—
summer and winter,
morning and evening,
birds coming back in spring,
the rivers carving valleys
and filling them up again,
seas rising and falling.
But what when the eye does not wake
to see or the heart to sing it?

How I begrudge the body's slow death;
would rather be siezed and eaten
by an eagle or a sharp fish
than by this inward worming.
Must we live at the last in a house with dirty windows
and doors that will not open,
the chimneys clogged and the hearthfire grown too sluggish
to make real flames anymore?
To desire nothing anymore
except sleep?
If one could only
spin some kind of a cocoon
and then wait mindless
as a caterpillar that winters on a bare branch.

*1963*

# Elements For
# An Autobiography

1.  The gold cowslip
    alluring far off
    at the center of the black muck
    she dared not wade through
    to touch.

2.  Coughing at night
    in the dark house
    with the curved bannister.
    The old patriarch
    lies asleep.
    They come at night warning her
    not to,
    not to wake grandfather.
    If she does not
    they will give her, they say,
    a shiny pin of silver
    shaped like a little boat.

3.  Mushrooms in the damp woods,
    lichens spreading
    over granite their
    rosy or leaf-colored
    longing for symmetry.

4.  Horses:
    the sweet smell of leather, the
    cold bit
    stained green,
    the long reins dragging
    behind her
    as she slyly creeps up
    to the wild hoofed one in the pasture.

*1971*

# Lament

Ancient camels
crossing a puddle of hot rock
left indelible footprints.

Your footprints still startle me
into aching recollection.

The tools left hanging in your workshop:
the little knife you gave me
like the one you always carried
wherever you were,
in the car, on picnics,
to open whatever needed to be opened,
to dig out splinters,
to tighten loose screws
when the world seemed to be falling apart.

It is the workman in you that I weep for:
the squares and levels,
saws all shapes and sizes,
nails for every imaginable place or purpose,
screwdrivers, nuts and bolts—
there was nothing you would not try
to make or mend.

You are gone now.
How often my own life seems past any mending.

*1975*

V.   from **The Ripened Fields**

# Whom God Hath Joined

And does God join through word of man?
Were we made one by priestly word?
By anything we said that day?
By anything we heard?

Were we made one by act of flesh,
by ancient hungers stirred and fed?
Why, then, the aching times we lay
lonely in marriage bed?

Why then the struggle and the tears,
the two in conflict ceaselessly,
oneness so perilously born
out of the you and me?

Oh, stranger far than book and ring
the woven oneness two may know
who from self's ruined battle ground
have watched their own hearts grow;

Who see, with wonder on their lips,
with eyes tear-cleansed and opened wide,
that struggle each for his own soul
was struggle side by side.

*1954*

# Ahsahta Press

## MODERN AND CONTEMPORARY POETRY OF THE WEST

*The Selected Poems of Norman Macleod*
Introduction by A. Thomas Trusky
ISBN 0-916272-00-1

*Gwendolen Haste, Selected Poems*
Preface by Carol Mullaney
ISBN 0-916272-01-X

*Peggy Pond Church, New & Selected Poems*
Introduction by T. M. Pearce
ISBN 0-916272-02-8

*A Taste of the Knife,* by Marnie Walsh
Introduction by John Milton
ISBN 0-916272-03-6
(available Fall, 1976)

*Nine Years After Bering,* by August Kleinzahler
ISBN 0-916272-04-4
(available Winter, 1977)


Please enclose payment ($2 per volume) with your order; for
handling and postage, please add 25¢ per volume.
Ahsahta Press • University Bookstore • Boise State University
1910 College Boulevard • Boise, Idaho 83725